piano · vocal · guitar

chart hits of 04-05

ISBN 0-634-09546-3

7777 W. BLUEMOUND RD. P.O. BOX 13819 MILWAUKEE, WI 53213

For all works contained herein:
Unauthorized copying, arranging, adapting, recording or public performance is an infringement of copyright.
Infringers are liable under the law.

Visit Hal Leonard Online at
www.halleonard.com

4	BABY IT'S YOU	JoJo featuring Bow Wow
7	BELIEVE (from *POLAR EXPRESS*)	Josh Groban
12	BREAKAWAY	Kelly Clarkson
26	DANGEROUSLY IN LOVE	Beyoncé
38	DARE YOU TO MOVE	Switchfoot
19	DIARY	Alicia Keys featuring Tony! Toni! Tone!
48	GIVE A LITTLE BIT	Goo Goo Dolls
53	HEAVEN	Los Lonely Boys
60	MY BOO	Usher & Alicia Keys
74	MY HAPPY ENDING	Avril Lavigne
67	1985	Bowling For Soup
80	ON THE WAY DOWN	Ryan Cabrera
86	OVER AND OVER	Nelly featuring Tim McGraw
98	PIECES OF ME	Ashlee Simpson
93	REMEMBER WHEN IT RAINED	Josh Groban
104	SHE WILL BE LOVED	Maroon5
120	SOMEBODY TOLD ME	The Killers
126	WHITE HOUSES	Vanessa Carlton
113	WORLD ON FIRE	Sarah McLachlan
136	YOU'LL THINK OF ME	Keith Urban

BREAKAWAY
from THE PRINCESS DIARIES 2: ROYAL ENGAGEMENT

Words and Music by BRIDGET BENENATE, AVRIL LAVIGNE and MATTHEW GERRARD

Copyright © 2004 Music Of Windswept, Friends Of Seagulls Music Publishing, Blotter Music, Almo Music Corp., Avril Lavigne Publishing Ltd., WB Music Corp. and G Matt Music
All Rights for Friends Of Seagulls Music Publishing and Blotter Music Administered by Music Of Windswept
All Rights for Avril Lavigne Publishing Ltd. Controlled and Administered by Almo Music Corp.
All Rights Reserved   Used by Permission

*Both times: Lead vocal sung at written pitch.

DANGEROUSLY IN LOVE

Words and Music by BEYONCÉ KNOWLES and ERROL McCALLA

DARE YOU TO MOVE

Words and Music by
JONATHAN FOREMAN

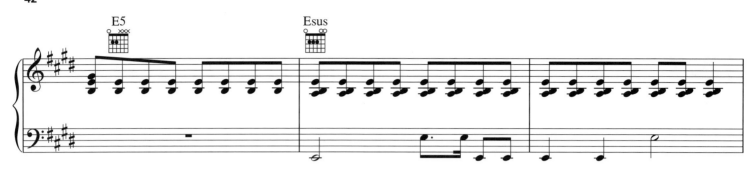
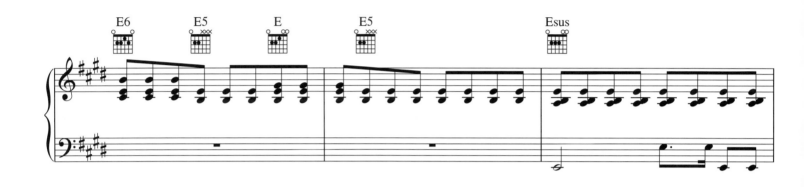
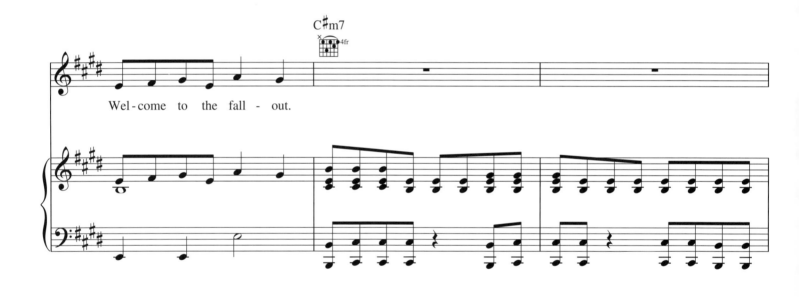

Wel-come to the fall-out.

Wel-come to re-sist - ance.

HEAVEN

Words and Music by HENRY GARZA, JOEY GARZA and RINGO GARZA

*Recorded a half step lower.

© 2003 EMI BLACKWOOD MUSIC INC., GARZA BROS. MUSIC and EITHER OR MUSIC
All Rights Controlled and Administered by EMI BLACKWOOD MUSIC INC.
All Rights Reserved   International Copyright Secured   Used by Permission

MY BOO

Words and Music by ALICIA KEYS,
JERMAINE DUPRI, TAURIAN SHROPSHIRE
and MANUEL SEAL

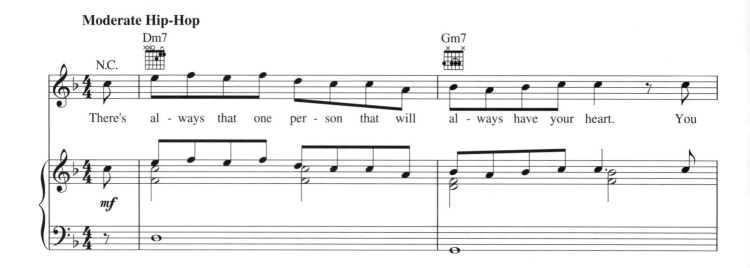
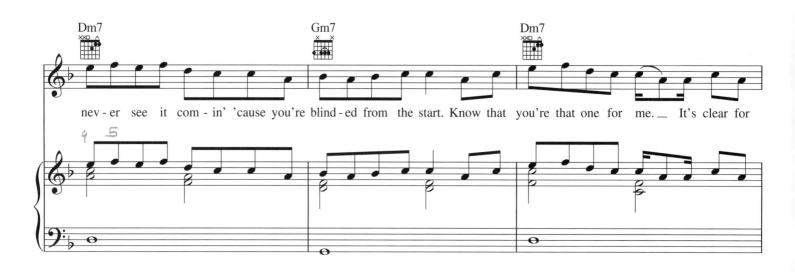
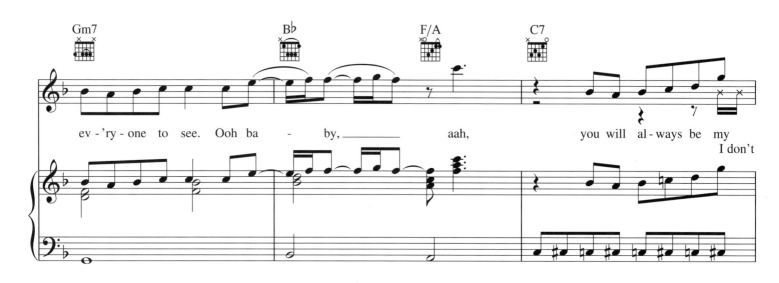

© 2004 EMI APRIL MUSIC INC., LELLOW PRODUCTIONS, SHANIAH CYMONE MUSIC, PHOENIX AVE MUSIC PUBLISHING,
JUSTIN COMBS PUBLISHING COMPANY, INC., BMG SONGS, INC. and SLACK A.D. MUSIC
All Rights for LELLOW PRODUCTIONS, SHANIAH CYMONE MUSIC, PHOENIX AVE MUSIC and JUSTIN COMBS PUBLISHING COMPANY, INC.
Controlled and Administered by EMI APRIL MUSIC INC.
All Rights for SLACK A.D. MUSIC Controlled and Administered by BMG SONGS, INC.
All Rights Reserved   International Copyright Secured   Used by Permission

1985

Words and Music by MITCH ALLEN, JOHN ALLEN and JARET REDDICK

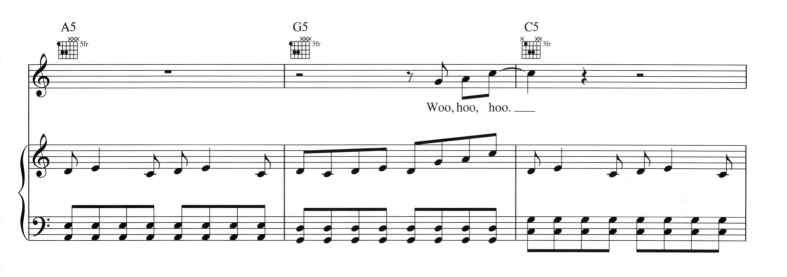

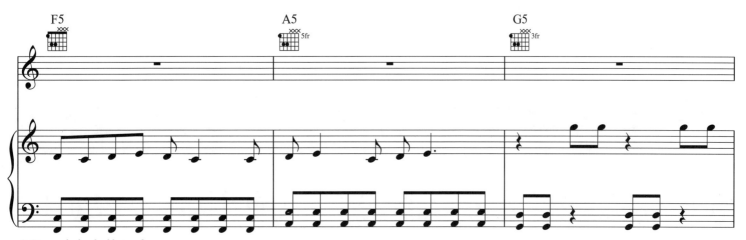

*Recorded a half step lower.

© 2004 EMI APRIL MUSIC INC., MATZOH-BALL MUSIC, EMI BLACKWOOD MUSIC INC., EASTSIDE JOHNNY NO-ASS MUSIC,
ZOMBA ENTERPRISES INC. and DROP YOUR PANTS PUBLISHING
All Rights for MATZOH-BALL MUSIC Controlled and Administered by EMI APRIL MUSIC INC.
All Rights for EASTSIDE JOHNNY NO-ASS MUSIC Controlled and Administered by EMI BLACKWOOD MUSIC INC.
All Rights for DROP YOUR PANTS PUBLISHING Controlled and Administered by ZOMBA ENTERPRISES INC.
All Rights Reserved   International Copyright Secured   Used by Permission

MY HAPPY ENDING

Words and Music by AVRIL LAVIGNE
and BUTCH WALKER

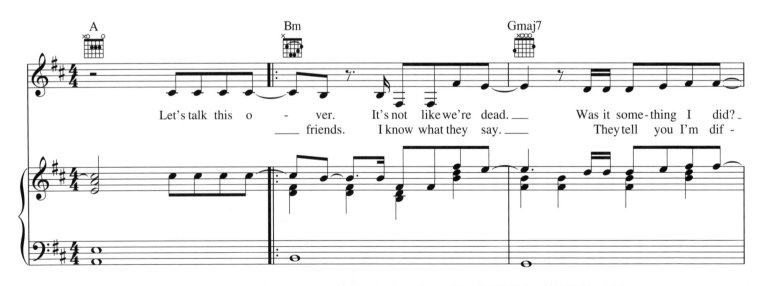

Let's talk this o - ver. It's not like we're dead. Was it some-thing I did?
_____ friends. I know what they say. _____ They tell you I'm dif-

Copyright © 2004 ALMO MUSIC CORP., AVRIL LAVIGNE PUBLISHING LTD., EMI BLACKWOOD MUSIC INC. and SONOTROCK MUSIC
All Rights for AVRIL LAVIGNE PUBLISHING LTD. Controlled and Administered by ALMO MUSIC CORP.
All Rights for SONOTROCK MUSIC Controlled and Administered by EMI BLACKWOOD MUSIC INC.
All Rights Reserved   Used by Permission

REMEMBER WHEN IT RAINED

Words and Music by ERIC MOUQUET
and JOSH GROBAN

PIECES OF ME

Words and Music by ASHLEE SIMPSON,
JOHN SHANKS and KARA DioGUARDI

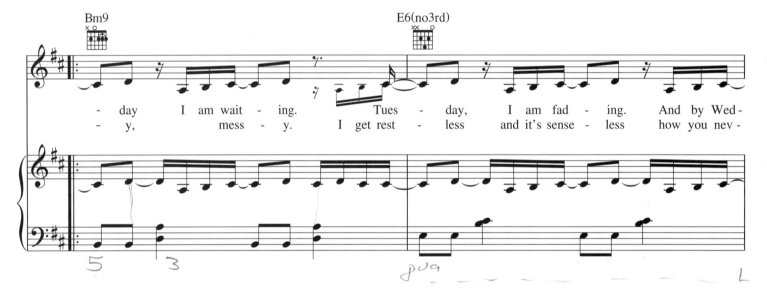
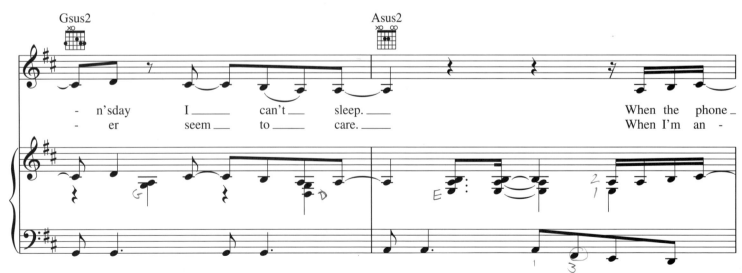

© 2004 EMI APRIL MUSIC INC., BIG A NIKKI, WB MUSIC CORP., DYLAN JACKSON MUSIC and K'STUFF PUBLISHING
All Rights for BIG A NIKKI Controlled and Administered by EMI APRIL MUSIC INC.
All Rights for DYLAN JACKSON MUSIC Controlled and Administered by WB MUSIC CORP.
All Rights Reserved   International Copyright Secured   Used by Permission

SHE WILL BE LOVED

Words and Music by ADAM LEVINE
and JAMES VALENTINE

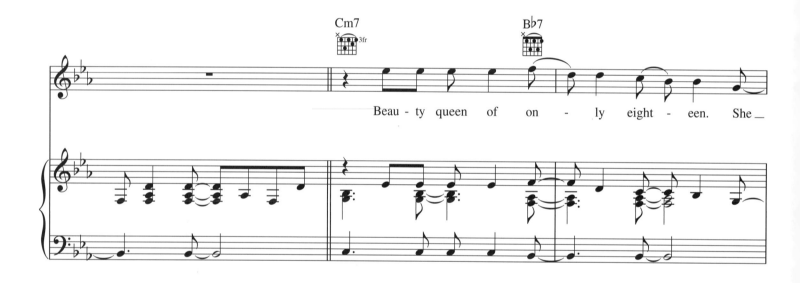

Copyright © 2002 by BMG Songs, Inc., Valentine Valentine, Careers-BMG Music Publishing, Inc. and February Twenty Second Music
All Rights for Valentine Valentine in the United States Administered by BMG Songs, Inc.
All Rights for February Twenty Second Music in the United States Administered by Careers-BMG Music Publishing, Inc.
International Copyright Secured   All Rights Reserved

WORLD ON FIRE

Words and Music by SARAH McLACHLAN
and PIERRE MARCHAND

2.14.06

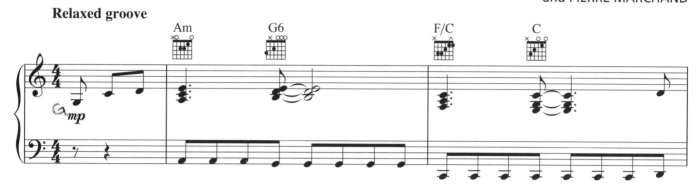
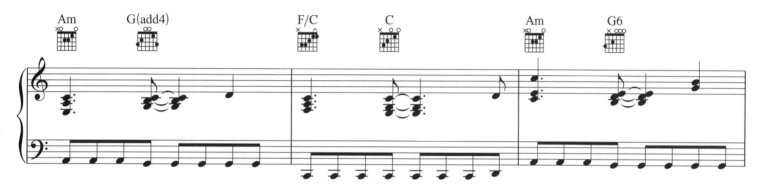

Hearts are worn in these dark ages. You're not a- lone in this
I watch the heav- ens for my fi- nal call- ing. Some- thing I can do to

Copyright © 2003 Sony/ATV Songs LLC, Tyde Music and Studio Nomade Music
All Rights on behalf of Sony/ATV Songs LLC and Tyde Music Administered by Sony/ATV Music Publishing, 8 Music Square West, Nashville, TN 37203
International Copyright Secured All Rights Reserved

SOMEBODY TOLD ME

Words and Music by BRANDON FLOWERS,
DAVE KEUNING, MARK STOERMER
and RONNIE VANNUCCI

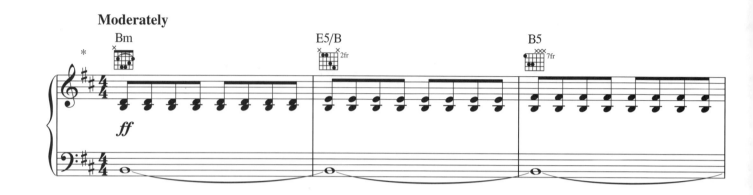

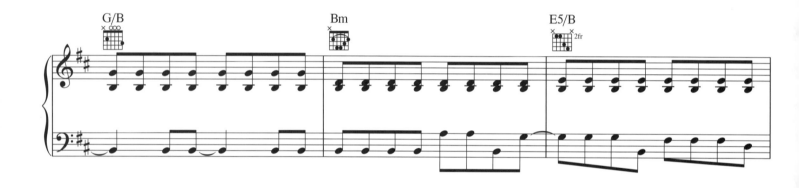

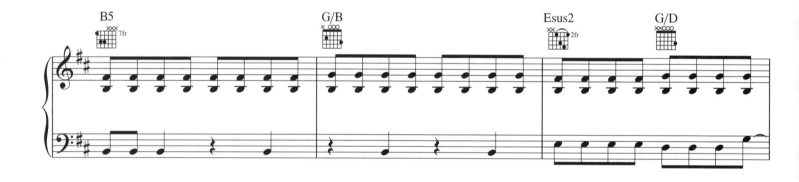

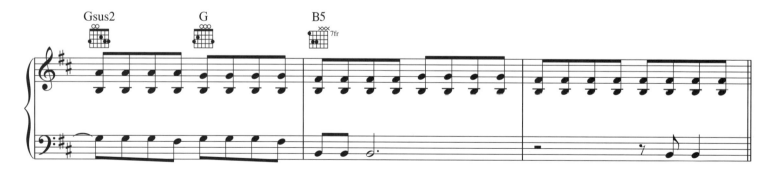

* Recorded a half step lower.

Copyright © 2004 UNIVERSAL MUSIC PUBLISHING LTD.
All Rights in the United States and Canada Controlled and Administered by UNIVERSAL-POLYGRAM INTERNATIONAL PUBLISHING, INC.
All Rights Reserved   Used by Permission

WHITE HOUSES

Words and Music by VANESSA CARLTON
and STEPHAN JENKINS

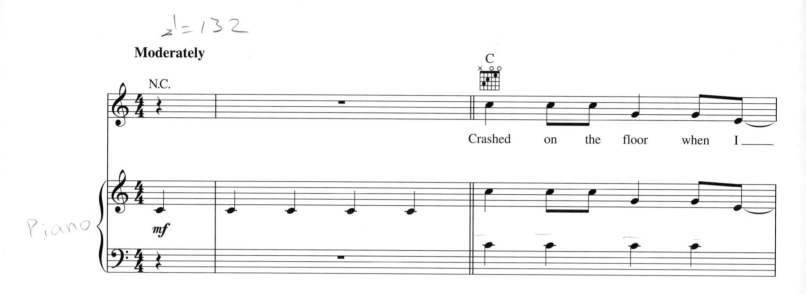

Copyright © 2004 SONGS OF UNIVERSAL, INC., ROSASHARN MUSIC and THREE EB PUBLISHING
All Rights for ROSASHARN MUSIC Controlled and Administered by SONGS OF UNIVERSAL, INC.
All Rights Reserved   Used by Permission

YOU'LL THINK OF ME

Words and Music by TY LACY,
DENNIS MATKOSKY and DARRELL BROWN

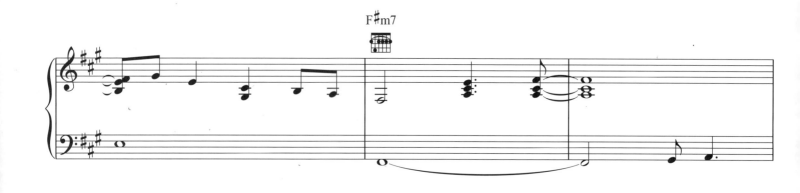

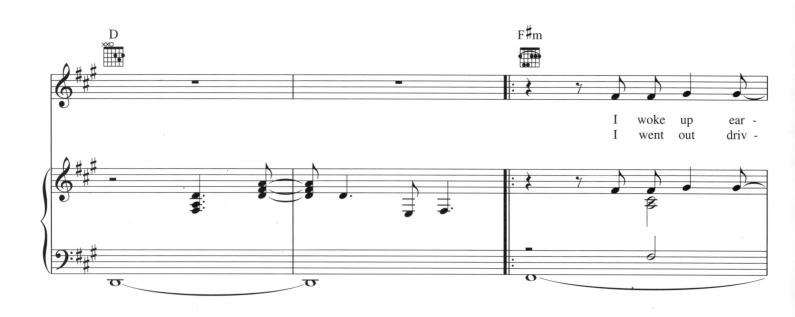

I woke up ear-
I went out driv-

© 2002 EMI APRIL MUSIC INC., TY ME A RIVER MUSIC, JESKAR MUSIC, ALMO MUSIC CORP. and ORIGINAL BLISS MUSIC
All Rights for TY ME A RIVER MUSIC and JESKAR MUSIC Controlled and Administered by EMI APRIL MUSIC INC.
All Rights for ORIGINAL BLISS MUSIC Controlled and Administered by ALMO MUSIC CORP.
All Rights Reserved   International Copyright Secured   Used by Permission